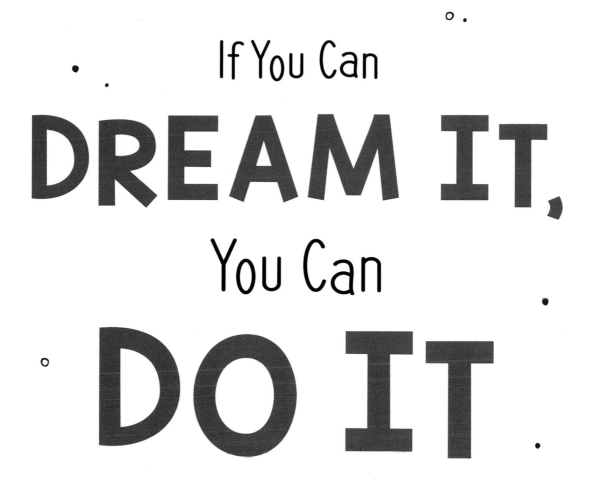

If You Can

DREAM IT,

You Can

DO IT

How 25 inspiring individuals found their dream jobs

COLLEEN NELSON & KATHIE MACISAAC

With illustrations by **SCOT RITCHIE**

pajamapress

First published in Canada and the United States in 2022

Text copyright © 2022 Colleen Nelson, Kathie MacIsaac

This edition copyright © 2022 Pajama Press Inc.

This is a first edition.

10 9 8 7 6 5 4 3 2 1

www.pajamapress.ca   info@pajamapress.ca

 Canada Council for the Arts   Conseil des arts du Canada

 ONTARIO ARTS COUNCIL
CONSEIL DES ARTS DE L'ONTARIO
an Ontario government agency
un organisme du gouvernement de l'Ontario

Canadä

The publisher gratefully acknowledges the support of the Canada Council for the Arts and the Ontario Arts Council for its publishing program. We acknowledge the financial support of the Government of Canada through the Canada Book Fund (CBF) for our publishing activities.

Library and Archives Canada Cataloguing in Publication
Title: If you can dream it, you can do it : how 25 inspiring individuals found their dream jobs /
    Colleen Nelson and Kathie MacIsaac ; with illustrations by Scot Ritchie.
Names: Nelson, Colleen, author. | MacIsaac, Kathie, author. | Ritchie, Scot, illustrator.
Description: First edition. | Includes index.
Identifiers: Canadiana 20220186154 | ISBN 9781772782288 (hardcover)
Subjects: LCSH: Success in business—Juvenile literature. | LCSH: Successful people—Biography—Juvenile
    literature. | LCSH: Vocational guidance—Juvenile literature. | LCSH: Occupations—Juvenile literature.
    | LCGFT: Biographies.
Classification: LCC HF5381.2 .N45 2022 | DDC j331.702—dc23

Publisher Cataloging-in-Publication Data (U.S.)
Names: Nelson, Colleen, author. | MacIsaac, Kathie, author. | Ritchie, Scot, illustrator.
Title: If You Can Dream It, You Can Do It / Colleen Nelson and Kathie MacIsaac ; with illustrations
    by Scot Ritchie.
Description: Toronto, Ontario Canada : Pajama Press, 2022. | Summary: "In this full-color, nonfiction
    resource, profiles of twenty-five diverse individuals share how each person got interested in their field,
    how they studied or trained for it, how others typically study or train for it, and their experience in
    their career. Informative sidebars share spin-off jobs, fun facts, pro tips about how readers can try
    out the field, and spotlight features about children who are doing just that. The book includes a table
    of contents, a glossary, an index, an interactive quiz, and reference pages about different types of
    education"— Provided by publisher.
Identifiers: ISBN 978-1-77278-228-8 (hardcover)
Subjects: LCSH: Occupations -- Biography-- Juvenile literature. | Job descriptions - Juvenile literature.
    | Vocational guidance - Juvenile literature. | BISAC: JUVENILE NONFICTION / Careers. | JUVENILE
    NONFICTION / Biography & Autobiography / General. | JUVENILE NONFICTION / Diversity
    & Multicultural.
Classification: LCC CT107.N457 |DDC 920.02- dc23

Cover and interior illustrations—Scot Ritchie
Book design—Lorena González Guillén

Printed in China by WKT Company

Pajama Press Inc.
11 Davies Avenue, Suite 103, Toronto, Ontario Canada, M4M 2A9

Distributed in Canada by UTP Distribution
5201 Dufferin Street Toronto, Ontario Canada, M3H 5T8

Distributed in the U.S. by Ingram Publisher Services
1 Ingram Blvd. La Vergne, TN 37086, USA

To my mom and dad
for encouraging me to believe
I could do anything

—C.N

For Emma, as she starts
her journey toward **her own dream job**

 —K.M.

CONTENTS

FOREWORD

The path to any dream job isn't simple, and there is no "right" way to get there. Some people discover their job by accident. For others, the job is a goal they are determined to achieve.

This book showcases **twenty-five inspiring people** who got their dream job. Through interviews, we learned about the education and training they needed, what they love about their job, and what advice they have for young people.

No matter who we interviewed, one thing was the same: there were bumps in the road. All the people we spoke with faced adversity, but they kept going. And every one of them still has other dreams they'd like to achieve.

We hope that as you read the profiles, you'll be inspired to follow your own dreams and find a job that fulfills and motivates you. We learned that a lot of young people don't let age or inexperience stand in their way, and you shouldn't either. It's never too early to follow your passion—and who knows? Maybe we'll be featuring **YOU** in our next book!

★ Colleen's Dream Job ★

I always wanted to be a *National Geographic* photographer! Traveling around the world and snapping pictures of unusual and hard-to-get-to locations seemed adventurous and exciting.

★ Colleen's Actual Job ★

I'm a teacher and I LOVE it! I can't think of a better job. Every day is different. I get to interact with young people and hopefully make a difference in their lives, whether that means changing how they think about themselves as readers and writers, or listening to them when they have a problem.

★ Kathie's Dream Job ★

I wanted to be a teacher, just like my mom.

★ Kathie's Real Job ★

I manage the children's department in a public library. I enjoy planning story times and organizing the summer reading program, but most of all, I love fostering a love of reading in young people.

GETTING SCHOOLED
Notes on Education and Training

Here's a quick guide to the different types
of education and training mentioned in this book.

Post-Secondary Education

Post-secondary education refers to any courses or degrees you get after high school.

The University Route

Every academic college or university offers baccalaureate, or bachelor's, degrees in a variety of areas. These take three to five years to complete. Some popular degrees include Arts, Sciences, Engineering, and Education. A bachelor's degree can be the first or final step in your post-secondary education. Sometimes people refer to this step in the journey as an "undergraduate" or "undergrad" degree.

People who complete their PhD are considered doctors even if they have no medical training.

A Doctor of Philosophy is not just for philosophers. The word means "love of wisdom."

Some students go on to "graduate school" or "grad school." A master's degree, which makes someone a master in their area of study, usually takes one year to complete. The highest level, a "Doctor in Philosophy" (PhD), requires an additional four to six years of coursework and research.

The Trade / Technical College Route

Trade and technical schools offer students the chance to get hands-on experience by partnering with industry experts. Students alternate between coursework and apprenticeships to gain the skills they need. These students graduate with a diploma or certificate and, more importantly, a marketable skill.

Some tradespeople, like carpenters, welders, automotive service technicians, plumbers, and heavy-duty equipment operators, also require certification to be accredited. They need to take an exam and complete training hours with an instructor.

On-the-Job Training

Post-secondary education isn't necessary for every job. Finding a mentor—someone who has experience and is willing to share their skills—is also an option. Some companies offer training through apprenticeships or internships.

Apprenticeships are generally longer (one to three years), while internships are less than a year. The salary is minimal, but getting an internship can result in getting hired.

MELISSA MÁRQUEZ

— Marine Biologist —

> 66 Be a part of nature, not apart from it. 99

As a kid growing up in Puerto Rico, Melissa spent a lot of time in the ocean. It was always her dream not just to learn about sea life, but to help others explore it. Melissa first went to college in Florida to get her bachelor's degree in marine biology. With this degree Melissa could have found many jobs related to the study of oceans, but her dream was to work on independent projects and teach at a university, so she crossed the world to continue her education: first to New Zealand for her master's and then to Australia for her PhD.

The most important part of being a marine biologist is asking questions and searching for truth. Like any good scientist, Melissa follows the **scientific method** to ensure her conclusions are not biased. Melissa spends a lot of time in the ocean, but just as much time in a lab, or at a computer, compiling her observations and making hypotheses to help guide her research. When she's got enough **data** to make a confident conclusion, she shares her findings with other marine biologists by writing a research paper.

PRO TIP

★ Spend time outdoors looking for unusual things in nature.

★ If you can't be in it, learn about it. Watch shows and read books about the natural world.

★ Promote sustainable actions. We can all do something to make the planet better.

OTHER WORK

Other fields of study in **MARINE BIOLOGY**:

★ **Ichthyology**, the study of fish

★ **Microbiology**, the study of microorganisms in water

★ **Environmental marine biology**, the study of the ocean's health

Before she became a marine biologist, Melissa was an avid watcher of Shark Week on the Discovery Channel. It was one of the things that inspired her to focus on sharks for her PhD. But she wondered why there weren't more female marine biologists. She set out to change that because, as she says, "You can't be what you can't see." Melissa's outreach efforts got her noticed and she became a host on Shark Week.

LIVING the DREAM

New Zealander **RILEY HATHAWAY** was twelve years old when she filmed a school project on sea turtles and plastic. Her dad, an underwater cameraman, realized how powerful kids teaching other kids about the ocean could be. Together, they began filming videos for their website, *Young Ocean Explorers*. Since then,  Riley and her dad have explored oceans around the world. She's had encounters with sea life, from orcas to stingrays to sharks. Riley has presented at TEDxAuckland and continues to share her stories about the ocean and the world that exists within it. Check out some of her videos on the Young Ocean Explorers website: **youngoceanexplorers.com**.

SPIN-OFF JOBS

★ Aquatic veterinarians specialize in the treatment and care of ocean animals.

★ Scuba-diving instructors teach people the safe and proper way to explore underwater.

★ Marine environment economists work with governments and private companies to protect marine life and manage resources.

★ WHY NOT TRY ★

Following a role-model scientist online. Melissa is at **www.melissacristinamarquez.com**

SUNIL GURMUKH
— Human Rights Lawyer —

> 66 The best part of my job as a human rights lawyer is helping create positive change for vulnerable people—to know that you made a real difference in people's lives. 99

When Sunil was a high school student, debating was a big part of his life. He enjoyed competing and arguing about different issues. He even advanced to the national debating finals at the age of seventeen. It's a skill he continues to practice in his job as a lawyer, but now he uses it to fight for equality and human rights. After receiving a university degree in business at Queen's University, Sunil took the LSAT, an entrance exam to get into law school. Once he graduated from law school at Western University, he spent another ten months doing on-the-job training called *articling*. At this time, he helped represent companies and police and was exposed to human rights law when someone complained that a police officer had discriminated against them because of their race. After articling, Sunil decided to be a lawyer who helps vulnerable people ensure they are treated with respect and dignity. In other words, to make sure they are not treated badly or differently because of who they are—their race, gender, disability, or sexual orientation for example (things that are part of their identity). He went to work at a legal clinic to help fight anti-Black racism before moving to the Ontario Human Rights Commission.

At the Commission, Sunil works as part of a team of individuals to address discrimination that affects lots of vulnerable people. They develop policies for people to understand their rights and for organizations to know their responsibilities.

★ WHY NOT TRY ★
Starting a social justice club at your school.

PRO TIP
Write letters to your government representatives to fight for human rights and lobby for change.

They engage in public education and go to court and the Human Rights Tribunal of Ontario to advance and promote human rights. Making new and unique arguments, or trying things that have never been done before, requires creative thinking. Sunil works with other lawyers and community groups to build the best arguments to win cases. He works with Commission team members responsible for communications and education to help find ways to promote and teach others about their work. He also meets with policymakers to encourage change.

Sunil's workday involves much more than arguing cases in court. Listening is an extremely important part of his job. He enjoys forming relationships with vulnerable people who share their stories and experiences with him. He does a lot of reading to learn how people have been treated in different situations. He educates people on their human rights and what actions they can take if they're mistreated. He also helps write policies, articles, and reports. In addition to his work as a lawyer, Sunil is a visiting **professor** at Western University's **Faculty** of Law. He loves teaching and recently taught a class on racism in policing. He is currently working with students on a research project on this topic.

Sunil says being a human rights lawyer is his dream job because he loves that his work helps people. He adds that anyone can be a human rights champion by calling out discrimination when they see it and speaking up for change in their communities. They can also listen and share what they learn to change the hearts and minds of the people around them.

SPIN-OFF JOBS

★ **Human resource professionals** make sure employees are treated fairly at work.

★ **Journalists** inform the public about injustices.

★ **Social workers** help individuals and families with challenges they face.

INSPIRING INDIVIDUALS

LARISSA CRAWFORD was sixteen when she started fundraising to support libraries in Canada and Ghana. She now runs her own company called Future Ancestors Services, which helps clients consider their impact on others and the environment. Her focus on Indigenous and anti-racism research and climate change taught her that understanding the past is the key to healing and to a better future for generations to come.

DAVID A. ROBERTSON

— Author —

66 Tell stories that matter. 99

David Alexander Robertson always knew he wanted to become a writer. He remembers running home from school with a book of ten poems his third-grade teacher had typed up for him. It was called "The Bestest Poems I Ever Wrote". He announced that day that he was going to be a writer.

It takes determination and practice—lots of practice—to write professionally. In university, Dave found **mentors** and professors who gave him feedback on his writing. Even now, he reads a lot and pays attention to what other writers do well. Writing every day is a big part of what helps a writer get better. Dave challenges himself by writing different genres and for different age groups. He's published picture books, graphic novels, and novels for middle-grade and young-adult readers. He's also written books for adults and

INSPIRING INDIVIDUALS

DAV PILKEY (author of the Dogman and Captain Underpants books), award-winning Canadian author Marsha Skrypuch, and author-illustrator Patricia Polacco all have a surprising thing in common. They have dyslexia, a learning difference which makes it difficult to learn to read, spell, and write. These authors didn't let anything stand in their way—and neither should you!

LIVING the DREAM

SARENA and **SASHA NANUA** have always loved books. The twin sisters ran a blog for many years and organized panels featuring their favorite young-adult authors. When they were nineteen years old they started writing a young-adult fantasy book. Four years later, *Sisters of the Snake* was published!

a memoir about his relationship with his father, which also became a podcast.

Some writers take creative-writing courses at university to improve their skills and to learn about different genres from experts. But it isn't necessary. Ultimately, becoming an author is about having the passion and determination to stick with a project.

Once a manuscript is completed, Dave sends it to a publishing company. If the acquisitions editor recommends it, Dave signs a **contract** and the manuscript moves on to the next stage: revisions. Revisions consume a lot of time, but they make an author's work better.

Some authors choose to self-publish, which is a non-traditional way to turn your manuscript into a book. It means the author is in charge of editing and marketing their own work. They pay all the costs of turning it into a book, but they also get all the profit.

Putting a story into the world is always a risk. Dave, who is Cree, hopes his stories will create change and educate people. Dave's books have been number one on national bestseller lists and won prestigious awards, like the Governor General's Award in Canada.

Even though most writers work alone at their computer, Dave's favorite part of being an author is when he can be with other people. He likes getting out to meet kids, teachers, and writers so he can share the joy of writing and hear their stories too.

PRO TIP

★ Enter writing contests

★ Find out if your public library has a writer in residence who will mentor aspiring writers

★ Look for courses at local writer's guilds

★ Start a blog about your favorite authors and books

★ Start a writing group

OTHER WORK

AUTHORS also:

★ Teach creative writing courses

★ Edit other writers

★ Write articles for magazines and newspapers

★ WHY NOT TRY ★

Keep a journal of ideas. You never know which one will grow into a story.

THERESA TAM
— Chief Public Health Officer of Canada —

❝ It's not entirely a scientific pursuit. It is about the human condition, it's about relationships with people, it's about the art of communication and listening. ❞

Theresa was passionate about both music and science when she was a kid. She played three different instruments, but she also loved looking through a microscope and learning how the human body worked. With her well-rounded interests, she had a good foundation for whatever career she chose to pursue.

Theresa's love and aptitude for science was encouraged by an inspiring role model: her secondary-school biology teacher. Although fewer women were practicing medicine in England in the 1980s compared to today, Theresa decided to earn her medical degree. But the more Theresa learned, the more she wanted to know. After she got her medical degree, she spent eight more years specializing in pediatrics to work with children, infectious disease, and field epidemiology (training to be a disease detective). This led to a career in public health.

Theresa is now Canada's Chief Public Health Officer, the federal government's top public health official. Her job involves understanding public health challenges and providing advice on how to handle them. She works with medical officers in each province and territory to protect and promote people's health. She also acts as a bridge between the public and the government officials who make decisions about health, such as the Minister of Health. Theresa says it's a very special responsibility

SPIN-OFF JOBS

★ **Biochemists** study diseases and help create new drugs to treat them.

★ **Nurses** care for patients and help them get well when they are sick.

★ **Medical lab technicians** run tests and analyze samples to determine what's wrong with a patient.

to advise individuals who have the power to make things happen.

During the COVID-19 pandemic, Theresa became much more visible to the public since one of her roles is managing public health emergencies. She needed to quickly understand the outbreak, how it started, who it affected, and how to prevent its spread. She also needed to figure out how to support people who got sick. Theresa says her role is like that of an orchestra conductor. She doesn't play all the instruments, but she has the score in front of her to see all the moving parts and how they come together as a whole to play a particular piece of music. The musicians in this example are experts in various fields, from mathematicians and economists to Indigenous leaders and vaccine researchers, and members of the public, including people just like you.

Theresa's job involves a lot of responsibility, but it's an exciting life. She loves to be involved in something important to the lives of Canadians. She travels and connects with people and communities around the country to promote health. One of her goals is to communicate with people of all ages about health-related issues that are relevant to them. Theresa learns something new every day and wants to have the biggest possible impact on the well-being of others.

PRO TIP

Be open to new opportunities, and don't be afraid to follow where they lead you.

★ WHY NOT TRY ★

Joining a science club at school or through a local university.

LIVING the DREAM

A project for a high-school science fair turned into groundbreaking research for seventeen-year-old **DASIA TAYLOR**. She soaked medical sutures in beet juice, which changes color when it's exposed to different **pH levels**. Since sutures are used to close wounds, and since the pH level of a patient's skin will increase when an infection begins, the color-changing sutures help detect infections before other symptoms appear. Dasia is currently patenting her idea, which could be used in regions with few resources to detect infection while it's still at a manageable stage. Though more research is needed, Dasia's idea can greatly impact people's health worldwide.

JESSIE ANDERSON

— Barber —

> 66 Being a barber is about listening and communicating with clients. 99

Jessie began cutting his own hair when he was seventeen years old. Although he enjoyed it, he didn't consider it as a career path until he saw a barber's chair in a thrift-store window. After a rough senior year of high school and some mental health struggles, he saw an opportunity in hair styling and enrolled at a beauty school that offered courses for both hairstylists and barbers.

> Depending on the college, hairstyling courses can take anywhere from six months to two years.

★ WHY NOT TRY ★

Offer to work a few hours in a salon folding laundry, cleaning, or stocking shelves. Find out if it's an environment you enjoy.

PRO TIP

Start a portfolio with photographs of your best looks. They can be hairstyles you've done on yourself, or on your family and friends.

At school Jessie learned the fundamentals, like shear cuts, clipper cuts, fades, and beard design. He used a mannequin at first, then moved on to hands-on training with clients who paid a discounted rate to get cuts from students. Before Jessie could graduate, he had to complete training hours under the direction of a fully licensed barber.

Barbers and stylists have to build a clientele base. They usually start by working as an assistant at a salon— shampooing clients' hair, doing laundry and light cleaning, stocking supplies, and working at the reception desk.

Jessie wasn't interested in working for someone else. He knew that wherever he worked wouldn't just be about cutting hair. He wanted to create a community that promoted inclusivity. As a transgender man, Jessie knew it was important to eliminate the gendered feelings about hair that are present in many salons. Owning a business comes with more responsibility, but it's a role Jessie was happy to take on, not just as a barber, but as a leader for social justice. His shop, Big Bro's Barbershop in Vancouver, British Columbia, was born. Today it's part of the Dresscode Project, which is a listing of salons and barbershops that are safer spaces for trans people. The list can be found at dresscodeproject.com

NEIJAE GRAHAM-HENRIES

LIVING the DREAM

When **NEIJAE GRAHAM-HENRIES'** brother realized barbering school wasn't for him, Neijae decided to give it a try—even though she was just seven years old!

After the six-week course, Neijae decided to use the skills she'd learned, like safety, cleanliness, clipper control, and hair strokes, to help others. She now often volunteers to give free cuts and shape-ups to people in underserved communities, kids in need, and the homeless.

SPIN-OFF JOBS

★ Make-up artists transform people's faces using cosmetics or special-effects makeup.

★ Estheticians are trained to do lots of different services to help people feel confident— whether it's manicures, eyelash extensions, or hair removal.

MAKING a DIFFERENCE

A growing number of salons see the need to cut and style hair in a way that won't damage the earth. Freshair Boutique in Winnipeg, Manitoba, is a certified green business. They recycle a large percentage of the waste produced in the store and use non-toxic products and refillable containers to eliminate waste. They also promote other zero-packaging products.

BRENDA HSUEH

— Farmer —

> 66 Farming is the opposite of boring. 99

Brenda became a farmer for three reasons. First, she was concerned about the environment. Second, Brenda loved food. Finally, her Chinese Baptist faith gave her an interest in social justice. She wondered why farmers were undervalued when they provided an essential service. After all, everyone in the world needs food to survive, right?

Some farmers work land that has been in their family for generations. Not Brenda. She made the choice to become a farmer after leaving a career in finance. To see if farming was right for her, she spent a summer volunteering at a learning farm. After two months in the dirt, she knew she'd found what she wanted to do.

Brenda's farm is small, so she and her husband are able to do most of the work themselves. They raise sheep and grow vegetables, which they sell at markets and directly to customers. Just like any business owner, Brenda has to focus on planning, budgets, and projections to make sure her farm will succeed.

Every day on the farm is different. Depending on the season, Brenda might have to seed, tend plants, weed, prepare soil, or transplant seedlings. She structures her

PRO TIP

★ Visit farms of all types in different locations to see the variety that exist.

★ Plant a vegetable garden. Even if you don't have a yard, you can grow one inside.

★ Take note of where your food comes from. How much is grown locally?

You don't need an agricultural degree to be a successful farmer, but many options are available. A bachelor's degree in agriculture allows someone to pursue a career in food science, food production, or public policy. Courses on farm management and technology are helpful if you're running a large industrial farm.

day in one- to two-hours blocks so the physical demands don't take a toll on her body. Some jobs, like deliveries and harvesting, can take all day.

Even though Brenda grew up in the city of Edmonton in an immigrant family with no experience around a farm, it didn't stop her from doing what she believed in. She learned what she knows from asking questions, taking advice, and experimenting. "Each farming season is like a lab experiment," she says. "There's always something to try."

Farming is about innovation and being able to think on your feet. Brenda likes to think of it as taking care of life: plants, animals, and people too, since everyone relies on what farms produce.

For Brenda, the best part of farming is being outside. Each day brings rewarding moments, whether it's the crunch of a fresh lettuce leaf, a crop that succeeded despite the odds, or holding a newborn lamb.

SPIN-OFF JOBS

★ **Food scientists** determine the nutritional content of food and what's safe to put in our bodies.

★ **Environmental engineers** combine different science fields to create systems that prevent things like soil erosion, deforestation, and pollution.

★ **Arborists** cultivate, manage, and take care of trees.

LIVING the DREAM

KATIE STAGLIANO planted a cabbage seed when she was nine years old and watched it grow into a forty-pound cabbage. She donated it to a local soup kitchen where it fed over 275 people! That experience led Katie to begin Katie's Krops, a community of people who grow and donate produce to people in need. Her program has branched out to day camps, community dinners, and an outdoor classroom at her flagship garden. Katie lives by her motto, "It only takes a seedling," and has inspired thousands of other people to do the same.

KATIE STAGLIANO

MARK ROBINSON

— Meteorologist / Storm Chaser —

> **"** I love being on air and being able to bring the natural world back to people. **"**

Like many kids, Mark was terrified of thunderstorms when he was young. His fear lessened when he watched a whole storm pass by while safely sheltered with his family at a local zoo. Later, when he was an adult, Mark's passion for exploring the natural world collided with his interest in extreme weather and he got hooked on storm chasing. He taught himself how storms worked, what they did, and how to find them. He would often send his footage to The Weather Network after he edited it, and they hired him to be their first reporter to do live updates when Hurricane Katrina struck the United States in 2005. But as much as Mark loved what he was doing, there's isn't a paying job called a "storm chaser," and very few people make money at it.

Mark was encouraged to study meteorology, so he took a four-year degree in atmospheric science at York University. Meteorologists use a lot of math and science to understand what's happening in the atmosphere and the impact it's going to have on the Earth. Mark learned to understand computer models that organize data from satellites and to read instruments that measure wind speed, atmospheric pressure, humidity, and temperatures, all of which are important when predicting the weather.

Mark knew he wanted to be a meteorologist who worked in the field, exploring and sharing what he learned with others. He pitched an idea to The Weather Network for a video series called "Storm Hunters." The network

PRO TIP

Spend time outdoors and explore the natural world. Don't be afraid to get your clothes dirty. You can learn more about what you discover by checking out a book at the library or doing online research.

★ WHY NOT TRY ★

Taking videos of the weather in your area and submitting clips to a local news station.

agreed. Since then Mark and a crew have traveled around the world, recording and sharing extreme weather for viewers to enjoy from the comfort of their own homes.

Mark's job has a performance aspect, so public speaking and communication skills are extremely valuable. He often interviews experts, like a conservation officer who might explain the impact of an ice jam on nearby communities. Every storm Mark witnesses adds to his experience, helping him spot patterns and predict what might happen next. He uses this information to help people prepare early for serious weather-related emergencies.

Mark feels lucky to have seen so much of the world at a young age, but there are still many things he wants to see. His bucket list includes witnessing a sandstorm, visiting the Amazon, and exploring Australia. He's passionate about his work and excited to continue sharing his adventures with viewers.

SPIN-OFF JOBS

★ **Broadcast meteorologists** predict the weather forecast and share it with the public.

★ **Climatologists** study weather over a long time (possibly months or years) to understand how climate changes.

★ **Videographers** record and edit footage of an event.

LIVING the DREAM

CHASE MILLER was five years old the first time he went storm chasing with his parents, who own a photo-tour business in Texas that offers storm-chasing adventures. He used his mom's phone to take videos of lightning from the backseat of the car. He knew that his parents understood storms and would keep him safe. In 2016, at age six, Chase was there when a type of spinning storm called a supercell spawned a dozen tornadoes near Dodge City, Kansas. Chase is now twelve, and he loves traveling around the country with his family. In the future, he would like to play a bigger role in the family business, teaching others to understand storms and to capture images of those powerful events.

SCOTT EDWARDS

— Ornithologist / Museum Curator —

66 It's really an opportunity to expose students to how amazing our planet is and how important it is we take care of it. **99**

When Scott was ten years old, a neighbor in New York City introduced him to birdwatching. Using a pair of binoculars, he quickly fell in love with looking at birds up close and matching them to their picture in a field guide. When Scott went to college to study biology, he volunteered at the Smithsonian National Museum of Natural History and learned how scientists work and learn about birds. He decided to become an ornithologist, a person who studies birds.

Scott's graduate research for his PhD in zoology focused on learning how animals and plants evolve over time and in different parts of the world. Once he earned his degree, he became a professor at Harvard University where he hired graduate students to help him continue his work. In addition to his research and teaching, he now mentors students and helps them do their own research on birds in his lab. Some topics of study include why some birds live in family groups and benefit each other, how birds fight disease when attacked by a virus, and how the same species of bird might differ from one country to another.

Scott is also the curator at the Museum of Comparative Zoology at Harvard. A typical day might find him teaching and mentoring students in the morning, then walking to the museum to work in the afternoon. As a curator, Scott collects items and creates displays about **biodiversity**. A natural

SPIN-OFF JOBS

★ **Avian veterinarians** specialize in caring for the health of birds.

★ **Wildlife rehabilitators** rescue injured birds and help them return to the wild.

★ **Birdwatching tour guides** show people the best places to look for birds in an area.

history collection is important because it helps us understand the plants and animals on our planet. It also helps us understand how our planet is changing. He wants people to see the beauty of our world, and to be aware of the issues we face so we can address them.

Since an ornithologist is a type of scientist, Scott attends many conferences. Scientists need to communicate what they discover, share information, and learn from each other's work. They often collaborate or work together. Writing papers for professional journals about their discoveries is another crucial part of a scientist's work. Scott also speaks to groups of people and must clearly explain complex ideas to a wide audience. He loves sharing his passion for birds and getting people excited about the natural world.

An especially rewarding part of Scott's job involves fieldwork. He travels around the world to study birds, and he loves meeting new people from different cultures. He is always asking questions. He knows there is still so much unknown about birds that he will never run of questions to ask.

★ WHY NOT TRY ★

Participating in the Christmas bird count organized by the Audubon Society. You can connect with other bird lovers and learn about the bird activity in your neighborhood.

INSPIRING INDIVIDUALS

Nineteen-year-old British-Bangladeshi birder **MYA-ROSE CRAIG** officially started counting birds at the age of four. In 2019, at the age of seventeen, she became the youngest person to spot 5,000 different species after traveling to all seven continents and over thirty-eight countries with her family. Mya-Rose, also known as Birdgirl, is now an ornithologist, naturalist, and environmentalist. She campaigns for equal access to nature, encouraging everyone to be able to enjoy birds, and stopping biodiversity loss. She recently published a book, *We Have A Dream*, where she highlights thirty young environmentalists of color from around the world. She is the youngest Briton to receive an honorary doctorate from the University of Bristol.

MARTHA SCHOPPE
— Smokejumper —

> **"** I get to work with people who also enjoy working hard and completing challenging tasks in the outdoors. **"**

Martha is one of a handful of women who jump out of airplanes and parachute into remote areas to fight wildland fires. She had a decade of experience working outdoor jobs before she spent one season managing invasive plants with the forest service. She was already trained to fight wildfires, but after seeing a couple of fires start, she decided to make it her job.

Martha spent six years as a seasonal firefighter during the summer months. She and other firefighters would contain (put a line around) a fire, control it (prevent the fire from moving past the line), and then put it out. Martha loved the physical and mental challenges of being a firefighter. After working on several kinds of crew, she applied to become a smokejumper—a job that would require the most extreme training and testing of her skill and strength.

The United States has nine federal smokejumper bases located throughout the western states with a total of around 450 jumpers. Each spring, every smokejumper must undergo rigorous training that tests their physical endurance and their parachuting skills. During a fire season, smokejumpers rotate between bases and smaller outstations, depending on where wildfires are burning. Anywhere from two to twenty-four smokejumpers will respond to a wildfire. Martha enjoys getting to work with firefighters from all over the country and mentoring **rookies**. She also likes leading crews and teaching fire training to small groups of people.

★ WHY NOT TRY ★

Take a wilderness survival course to learn skills you need in the outdoors.

PRO TIP

Stay healthy and strong, and actively participate in outdoor activities.

Smokejumpers are responsible for making and repairing their own gear, which includes jump pants, jackets, and backpacks. The clothing is made of padded Kevlar, the same material used to make bullet-proof vests. When Martha is in the air ready to jump, she carries 100 pounds of extra weight from all her supplies and gear. The crew in the aircraft drop the remainder of the gear—food, water, and firefighting tools—by parachute after she lands. All this gear ensures Martha can be self-sufficient for seventy-two hours. She must quickly retrieve it and get to work.

Each fire differs due to **topography**, weather, and vegetation type, so Martha never knows what will be required until she arrives on the scene. She may need to clear access for ground crews to arrive. If a firebreak is necessary, she needs to cut down trees and clear brush. Sometimes she must dig a fire-line. She has to be prepared to work in wet, dry, smoky, and buggy conditions for hours at a time.

When she isn't fighting a fire, Martha spends time packing cargo boxes, maintaining and fixing equipment, exercising, and making sure she is prepared to respond immediately to the next call. Sometimes she reads or cooks. She has very few days off, but she's required to take at least one day off every three weeks.

Once fire season slows in the fall, Martha is free until next spring. Since wildland firefighters often work a year's worth of hours in just six months, they can take time off for family, travel, and adventure during the off-season. Martha's job requires her to be in excellent shape, so she stays active, competing in running races, ice climbing, skiing, and traveling.

Martha still has so much to learn about being a smoke-jumper. Parachuting skills, sewing, manufacturing, and repairing gear require a lot of practice. Martha loves her job and plans to stay fit enough to be a smokejumper for many years to come.

SPIN-OFF JOBS

★ **Helicopter pilots** drop water or chemicals on a forest fire to help contain it.

★ **Flight paramedics** provide medical assistance aboard aircraft, often in remote locations.

★ **Fire ecologists** study how wildland fires start as well as their relationship with the environment and animals around them.

FUN FACT
While most skydivers jump from around 14,000 feet above ground level, smokejumpers parachute from airplanes at only 3,000 feet. Their job is to get quickly to the ground so they can get to work.

RYOJI AMAMOTO

— Neuroscientist —

> 66 To discover something that nobody's ever known before is very gratifying. 99

Ryoji didn't like science in high school. He thought it was boring to memorize a lot of facts. He couldn't see why it was necessary or how it related to the real world. But a biology course in college gave him a chance to perform experiments and do hands-on learning. Once Ryoji saw that science could be more about discovering things than memorizing them, he was hooked. He pursued graduate studies at Harvard University, learning how salamanders and axolotls regenerate their limbs and how that affects their brains. If scientists could understand how some living creatures can regenerate parts of their bodies, maybe they could apply it to human brains affected by **degenerative** diseases like Parkinson's or Alzheimer's. Ryoji was excited about the potential of his work to help treat specific illnesses.

Once he obtained his PhD in developmental and regenerative biology, Ryoji decided to spend another five to six years doing experimental science as a **post-doctorate fellow**. By 2021 he was employed by a lab at Harvard performing experiments on mice to study **retinal** regeneration. When the cells in the eye break down due to genetic diseases such as retinitis pigmentosa, vision loss can result. Ryoji hopes that what he learns in his experiments can be used in the future to help regenerate cells and prevent or reverse vision loss.

One of the biggest misconceptions about scientists is that they spend their time working alone in a lab. Ryoji says this stereotype only relates to a small portion of what scientists do. They also give talks and speeches, attend conferences, and share information with scientists and the public to educate people about what they and their colleagues are learning. To obtain grants and funding to support more research, scientists need to sell themselves and the value of their work, so communication skills are very important. It's a slow process to run tests, wait for results, analyze data, and have enough conclusive evidence to write a paper to share results, but it's essential work. Ryoji spends a lot of time reading such papers to see what other scientists have discovered.

While collaboration and learning from each other is important, one goal of Ryoji's fellowship is to prove he can work independently. Once his fellowship is complete, he can start applying for a faculty position to get his own lab and become a professor. Ryoji hopes that one day he will make a drug that receives FDA approval for use in humans to treat a **neurodegenerative** disease and improve the lives of others.

PRO TIP

Apply to a research university (rather than a liberal arts college) if you're interested in science, as they have more opportunities to work in a lab.

★ WHY NOT TRY ★

Arranging a tour of a lab at a local university or college to learn more about the work they do.

LIVING the DREAM

AMOY ANTUNET

discovered her love for science at the age of three when she found her father's microscope. She started to make informational science videos that her father posted on Facebook, and they went viral. She explained concepts like how **neurotransmitters** work when she was only six years old! She's appeared on numerous television programs, and her enthusiasm for science (particularly neuroscience) is contagious. Amoy is now eleven years old and is interested in becoming a neurosurgeon. You can find out more about her at **amoyantunet.com**

SPIN-OFF JOBS

★ **Life science consultants** work with biotech or pharmaceutical companies to help them solve specific research-related problems.

★ **Science journal editors** review manuscripts, assess their quality, and send them to other researchers in the field to be assessed.

★ **Neurosurgeons** specialize in operating on the brain and spinal cord.

RABIA KHOKHAR

— Teacher —

> 66 Teaching is about working to create a better space for all people. 99

As a young child, Rabia would line up her stuffed animals to play school with them. She loved learning and always asked lots of questions. However, as a newcomer to Canada from Pakistan, she didn't see anyone who looked like her working in schools. It made her wonder if her dream job was possible. But her passion for teaching pushed her to pursue a career in education.

To get a bachelor's degree in education, a student must apply to a university's faculty of education, which is often a two-year program. Acceptance may be based on grades, volunteer work, an essay, or an interview. Often, an applicant needs to have completed a three-year undergrad degree first.

Part of learning to be a teacher is the **practicum**, or student teaching, which is arranged by the faculty. Rabia got hands-on experience under the guidance of a cooperating teacher. She observed lessons and then took the lead on preparing materials and teaching classes. Each practicum experience broadened Rabia's understanding of how good teachers manage classrooms, plan lessons, and assess their students.

Rabia sees herself as an activist as much as a teacher. In her role as a teacher-librarian, she strives to make the school a better space for everyone. Creating a fair and inclusive world through interactions with students and staff is always Rabia's priority.

Teaching means long days! She arrives to work 60–30 minutes before the first bell to prepare for her day and to

SPIN-OFF JOBS

★ **Education Directors** at museums develop lessons and tours for school groups.

★ **Community Literacy Outreach workers** visit families and work on early literacy skills with young children.

★ **Early Childhood Educators** work in daycares and preschools.

set up resources. Throughout a school day, Rabia works with whole classes, small groups, and individual students. She also collaborates with teachers to prepare lessons. Lunchtime is often spent supervising clubs, answering emails, or marking. Her day doesn't end when the students leave the building. She often stays late prepping for the next day, setting up displays, or meeting with parents and staff.

Rabia's advice to young people who want to be teachers is to open their eyes to the world around them and think about how small actions can make a big difference in a student's life. As Rabia says, "Teaching isn't just a job, it's a commitment to making the world a better place."

PRO TIP

Look for places to volunteer. Rabia volunteered at after-school clubs and with library reading programs, and taught Sunday school at her mosque.

GO GLOBAL

There are schools around the world, and they all need teachers! Gaining experience at a school overseas allows a teacher to travel and see other countries. You may be hired by the school itself, or by an agency that connects teachers to jobs. The hard part might not be getting a job, but deciding which international location is right for you!

INSPIRING INDIVIDUALS

Over thirty years ago, **MOHAMMED REZAI** arrived in Winnipeg, Canada, from Iran. He didn't know English and had no family or friends. In order to learn the language, he took English courses at Isaac Newton School. He credits his first English teacher, June Shymko, with inspiring him to believe in himself. Eventually, he became a teacher and, many years later, the principal of Isaac Newton— the first school he'd attended in his new country.

★ WHY NOT TRY ★

Working with younger kids in your school. You can be a reading buddy or offer to play games at lunch. **Be a leader!**

LEAH HEXTALL

— Play-by-Play Commentator —

> 66 If you see it, you know that it's possible to be it. And if we don't have little girls and little boys seeing women doing certain things, then there is no dream. 99

Leah always knew she wanted a career in the spotlight, but it wasn't until she combined her passion for hockey with entertaining others that she realized she wanted to go to school to become a sports broadcaster. She took a one-year diploma program in broadcasting performing arts and went on to work with three different networks, even hosting and reporting rinkside for Hockey Night in Canada.

After cutbacks left her without a job, Leah needed to reinvent herself. Her dream was to cover an Olympic Games in hockey, and she realized the way to stand out was to become a play-by-play commentator. She sought advice from experts in the field. She started going to American Hockey League (AHL) games and calling the game to herself while recording it on her phone. She attended practice skates to talk to players before the game. Since many networks hire their own announcers, Leah could use her connections to find opportunities to start calling games. She worked as a freelance commentator until being hired as an NHL play-by-play commentator for ESPN in 2021.

Leah had to learn a new set of skills than the ones she used before in sports broadcasting. She watched a lot of hockey to learn about the teams and players. She reached out to general managers, coaches, scouts, and teams' public relations people to learn about unique storylines, injuries, and what teams were working on. She had to memorize all

SPIN-OFF JOBS

★ **Broadcast producers** oversee the creation of on-air content.

★ **Sports camera operators** record and broadcast live sporting events.

★ **Radio announcers** share music and information with listeners.

the names and numbers of players for all thirty-two NHL teams. And she needed to share that information in real time while following what was happening on the ice.

Leah shares the broadcast booth with a color commentator, who explains the plays to the audience during a game. Usually this is a former professional hockey player who has inside knowledge of the sport. They are both supported by a person who tabulates statistics about the game and the league in general.

Leah finds her work challenging and thrilling. It inspires her to continually find new ways to tell a story that's interesting for the audience. She sees her job as that of a storyteller who expresses emotions using her voice and keeps the game exciting. Just like the fans, Leah doesn't know what's going to happen next, but she loves to bring a voice to the game for the audience.

In March of 2020, Leah was the first woman to call play-by-play for an NHL game. Now it's something Leah does regularly. It's important to her to open doors for more women to follow in her footsteps. When she looks at how much she has accomplished in the past few years, she can't wait to see what other opportunities wait for her in the future.

ISMAIL FERDOUS

— Documentary Photographer —

> **❝** You have to believe in your talent and nurture it. **❞**

In order to buy his first camera, Ismail Ferdous asked to borrow money from his dad. His father agreed on one condition: Ismail had to promise not to take photography too seriously. Ismail laughs at the memory because, as an award-winning photographer, he's glad he broke that promise!

Ismail started taking photos in his hometown of Dhaka, Bangladesh. He traveled around the city capturing images that were more than just pretty pictures. He wanted to tell stories, like the photojournalists he followed online. With his curiosity about the world and his interest in social justice issues, Ismail knew this was the kind of photography he was meant to do.

Like other careers in the arts, becoming a professional photographer combines technical skills, creativity, and business sense. Someone interested in photography might go the university route and get a fine arts degree; or, if they want to be a photojournalist like Ismail, they might get a degree in journalism.

On-the-job training is an essential part of becoming a professional photographer. Ismail started by joining a photography club where he went to seminars and organized exhibits. Eventually, his talent was noticed. He won a **scholarship** to a course in Washington, D.C., and then was hired as an assistant to a *National Geographic* photographer. It was the chance he'd been waiting for and now, years later, Ismail's own work can be found in magazines and newspapers around the world, including *National Geographic!*

When he is actively researching a story, Ismail will talk to people and connect with local journalists to find a protagonist, or subject. Then Ismail spends time building a relationship with the protagonist. Some of his photo documentaries have taken years of dedication, but the payoff has been international attention and **accolades** that raise his profile as a documentary photographer.

Ismail believes that committing to the lifestyle is essential. He would love to take his photographs a step further and make a film or a documentary. New ideas are always exciting when, as he says, "Storytelling is at the heart of it."

LIVING the DREAM

HAWKEYE HUEY, at four years old, was the youngest person ever published in *National Geographic*. His dad gave him his first camera during a father-son trip. The shots Hawkeye took impressed his dad and lots of other people too! His child's-eye view of the world was fresh and different. Hawkeye has gone on to do more shoots for *National Geographic* and *Vogue*, and his photos have been compiled in a book. He has over 175,000 followers on Instagram.

DID YOU KNOW?

National Geographic magazine runs a photography camp for young people from underserved communities, including at-risk and refugee teens. Top-notch photographers teach participants how to use photography to tell their stories and explore the world around them. You can view some of the photographs at **nationalgeographic.org/projects/photo-camp**

SPIN-OFF JOBS

★ Picture editors narrow down the photos received by a publication, selecting the best ones and suggesting retouches.

★ Gallery curators work with artists to stage exhibits. If the curator works for a museum, the purpose of the exhibit is to teach. At a private gallery, a curator is hoping to sell the art for the artist.

★ Retouchers work with the fine details on a photograph, using computer technology to enhance the image for publication.

★ WHY NOT TRY ★

Capturing not just a moment, but a story with photographs. Consider who your protagonist is and what story you want to tell.

SHAWN MAKEPEACE

— Animal and Conservation Interpreter —

> **"** Open your mind. You might have to do a lot of trial and error, but you can figure it out. **"**

When Shawn was twelve, an encounter with a dolphin at the Minnesota Zoo sparked a passion that shaped the rest of her life. She spent hours reading and learning more about dolphins. When she was diagnosed as legally blind at seventeen, she developed a keen interest in echolocation and how dolphins communicate using sound waves. Shawn went to graduate school and got a doctorate focused on Hearing and Animal Science. She found it difficult to find a job working with dolphins, so she started volunteering at the Saint Louis Zoo. She's now part of the staff as an animal and conservation interpreter.

Shawn's job requires her to talk with the zoo's guests rather than simply present information to them. She wants people to have an interactive and positive experience. She visits different habitats and has conversations about the animals that live there. She must be very knowledgeable because she never knows what kind of questions guests will ask her. She also needs to communicate information in accurate and meaningful ways for all age groups.

Shawn loves sharing her passion for animals, and she also passes along a conservation message. It's a highlight of her day when she feels she helps a guest care enough about the animals to take action to save them. She encourages people to recycle more and use sustainable products that won't hurt the environment.

Shawn's guide dog, Shonda, goes everywhere with her. Shonda has learned to ignore most of the zoo animals,

although she loves the river otters. Some animals, like the orangutans, will come right up to the glass and stare at Shonda. It's an excellent opportunity for Shawn to teach guests about guide and service dogs as well as zoo animals.

There is still bias and discrimination in jobs for people with a lack of vision. Shawn says volunteering can help a person get their foot in the door so others can see how capable they are and consider them for future job openings. She plans to further her training as an interpreter to better teach people about animals and make them care enough to protect their futures.

★ WHY NOT TRY ★

Volunteering at a zoo to learn more about animals and about how zoos operate.

LIVING the DREAM

JESSICA WALKER was researching empathy for a science-fair project when she learned about the short and horrific lives of some farm animals. With the support of her family, she turned her large backyard into the Little Red Barn Micro Sanctuary. Her first rescues were two piglets named George and Lucy. Then came a  dairy cow and two sheep. In 2020, she saved 5,000 laying chickens. Jessica works hard to give each animal a quality life, either at her sanctuary or at a new home. Jessica relies on her family's support, fundraising, and the expertise of a vet to create individualized care plans. Tours of the sanctuary show visitors that animals are someone, not something, which is the cornerstone of Little Red Barn's mission.

SPIN-OFF JOBS

★ **Zookeepers** feed and care for animals and maintain their enclosures.

★ **Zoo curators** find new animals for the zoo. They are also responsible for overseeing breeding programs, ensuring habitats are suitable for each type of animal, and providing them with healthy foods to eat.

★ **Exotic animal trainers** study how animals act and teach them to repeat specific behaviors.

EUGENIA CHENG

— Mathematician —

> 66 Ask yourself, in a dream world, what would I really want to do? Then do it! 99

Mathematician Eugenia Cheng makes time every day to "dream." That's what she calls the hour or so she spends at her kitchen counter scribbling ideas in her notebook. To Eugenia, math is less about numbers and more about abstract ideas and how they interact with each other.

Eugenia loves researching and communicating mathematical ideas and received her PhD from the University of Cambridge. After working as a professor in England, Eugenia moved to the United States and got a job at the University of Chicago. This move gave her the freedom to pursue new ways to share her love of math through writing, public speaking, and filming YouTube videos.

Eugenia's days vary wildly—just how she likes it. After her dreaming hour, she might work in her role as a teacher or a writer. There is always time set aside for answering emails and doing administrative work. Eugenia's job as a mathematics professor and author also involves traveling to give presentations at other schools and universities.

SPIN-OFF JOBS

★ **Operations Research Analysts** look for problems in how a company or business is run and offer solutions.

★ **Cryptanalytic Diagnosticians** analyze and decode signals or data, possibly to help with cyber or national security issues.

OTHER WORK

A few other **MATHEMATICIAN** jobs:

★ codebreaker for the National Security Agency

★ data analyst for a government agency

★ writing articles for magazines and newspapers

Being a mathematician isn't just about numbers. It's about solving problems and finding new ways to understand math. Eugenia often collaborates with other mathematicians to explain new ideas. Together, they organize and sort information, then draw conclusions. In her research, Eugenia uses math to help people understand the world. Difficult discussions, like gender inequality, can be explained and maybe solved by looking at data and making decisions based on statistics, not assumptions.

Eugenia's favorite thing about her job is taking the mystery out of math and helping people understand things they find difficult. As Eugenia says, "Math isn't about memorizing, it's about understanding."

PRO TIP

★ Watch math videos on YouTube. Eugenia has lots: **eugeniacheng.com/math/videos**

★ Look for math in the world around you. Math is about understanding something complex through structure. Do a puzzle, observe nature, learn a musical instrument, solve a problem.

LIVING the DREAM

When **YASHA ASLEY** was thirteen, he was contacted the University of Leicester. A panel had seen his work and wanted to know if he'd be interested in joining them as a math tutor while pursuing his degree in math. It meant he'd have to help people much older than him. A math **prodigy**, he was up for the challenge! He graduated with a degree in mathematics at fourteen and has continued his education by studying for a PhD.

FUN FACT

Want to win a million dollars? In 2000, the Clay Mathematics Institute offered a million-dollar prize for anyone who could correctly solve one of the seven outstanding problems in mathematics. Only one has been solved so far!

JOSHUA JONES
— Interior Designer —

> 66 Don't doubt your own abilities. 99

Joshua Jones' interior design work has been featured in magazines, and he has a long list of happy clients. For Joshua, who is Deaf, "design is about seeing, touching, and feeling—it has nothing to do with hearing." That's why starting an e-design company made a lot of sense. JJones Design Co. provides the same services as a traditional interior designer, but working with clients via email eliminates communication barriers. Interior designers consider the function of a space, the behavior and budget of the client, and, most importantly, safety codes. The aesthetic choices of how the room will look are based on client needs and preferences.

The first step to becoming an interior designer is to get a bachelor's degree in interior design. Course work includes design

★ WHY NOT TRY ★

Check out show homes in your area. Once or twice a year, home builders put newly built homes on display for the public. Touring them is a great way to see what's new in design and even make connections with local design firms.

While Joshua started his own company and focuses on residential design, there are other types of **INTERIOR DESIGNER**:

★ Corporate designers: create designs for professional workplaces that project the right image for the company

★ Sustainable designers: make sound environmental decisions when designing a space

★ Commercial designers: focus on hotel, restaurant and retail spaces that promote a positive customer experience

theory, computer aided design (CAD), and the structural (mechanical, electrical, and plumbing) and architectural elements of design. Students get hands-on experience doing studio projects, which are discussed and graded by their instructors. Some people continue their education in a master's program. To become an **accredited** interior designer, you must take an internationally recognized exam. Requirements to be considered a professional interior designer vary by region. Whether it's e-design or traditional in-person design, the process is the same: a designer begins by setting the project goals. For Joshua that means getting a sense of what his client wants. The next step is data collection. Joshua asks clients to send photos of their current space and to fill out a survey so he gets an understanding of their style and the function they need the room to provide. He encourages them to create a Pinterest board of room designs they like. The next stage is conceptualization. Interior designers provide their client with a detailed construction drawing, as well as a visualization, which can be anything from a hand-drawn illustration to a computer-generated 3-D rendering.

Joshua is a firm believer that individuals are in charge of their own success. He was patient and persistent and, after three years, started to see the results of his hard work. Today, JJones Design Co. is a successful e-design business with a growing list of clients.

SPIN-OFF JOBS

★ **3-D rendering artists** focus on translating a designer's plans into a 3-D computer image for clients.

★ **Set designers** create the on-stage spaces for movies, TV shows, and live theater.

★ **Interior decorators** make choices about the look and feel of a room. Unlike interior designers, they don't have the architectural training to change anything structural.

MAKING a DIFFERENCE

Mango Design Co is an interior design firm led by **TANYA MCLEAN** in British Columbia with a focus on balancing design and environmentally friendly practices. Tanya sources materials from local suppliers, searches for natural and eco-friendly materials, recycles construction materials, and installs alternate energy systems, like solar or geothermal.

CHRISTA BRUNEAU-GUENTHER

— Restaurant Owner / Chef —

> 66 I absolutely love feeding people; I think food is very powerful. It's meaningful, it represents community, family, nourishment, and medicine. 99

There were signs from an early age that Christa had the spirit of an **entrepreneur**. She was always on the lookout for ways to work and make money. She collected fallen fruit from the neighborhood trees to sell, babysat, and had a paper route. When Christa was fifteen, she started working in a small motel and restaurant where she learned to do all the different jobs in the kitchen. Her passion for cooking intensified when, in her early twenties, she opened a licensed daycare targeting inner-city families. Due to poverty, some of the children she served had poor diets, so she developed healthy recipes and applied for extra funding to send dinner home with their caregivers.

At this point, Christa, a Métis woman, began to develop a passion for traditional Indigenous foods. Her experience in the kitchen and with budgeting, grocery shopping, and gardening helped prepare her to eventually open her own restaurant called Feast Café Bistro in Winnipeg, Manitoba.

As a business owner, Christa needs to know how to do each job required to run her restaurant. She creates and cooks her recipes, hires staff and teaches them their roles, organizes the kitchen, provides customer service, manages the finances, and much more.

★ WHY NOT TRY ★

Volunteering at a soup kitchen to understand how your community helps feed individuals who are experiencing **food insecurity**.

40

It's also extremely important to Christa to make a difference in her community and to be mindful of the environment. She provides job opportunities for people who may have barriers to employment. She donates food to help feed the homeless. She uses takeout and catering items that are primarily compostable. She also tries to use locally sourced products. Christa is happy that her business can have a positive impact on the lives of others.

What's next? Christa would like to see more people cooking in their kitchens, a basic skill that many people lack today. Cooking can lead to a job, a career, or a business idea! Christa hopes to one day share more of her food knowledge to help others learn to grow, preserve, cook, garden, and enjoy healthy foods at home. She continues to follow her passion, focuses on what she's good at, and trusts the result will be a bright future.

SPIN-OFF JOBS

★ Butchers cut and sell meat to individuals and businesses.

★ Dieticians teach people about food and how to eat healthily.

★ Sous chefs are a head chef's primary assistants.

INSPIRING INDIVIDUALS

JULIAN FREDERICK was three when he asked to make his own birthday cake. As his passion for cooking grew, he wanted to share it with other young people. When he was twelve, he launched his own business, The Step Stool Chef, to teach cooking classes and sell products just for kids. Julian's goal is to make cooking fun and to empower kids to work independently in the kitchen. He is also a cookbook author and a popular speaker. Julian is especially interested in helping other kids start their own businesses.

PRO TIP

Spend time in the kitchen learning basic skills, like operating a mixer or slicing vegetables. Prepare simple meals like scrambled eggs or sandwiches.

feast

DR. RAPHAEL MALBRUE

— Veterinarian —

" Expect the unexpected! "

When Raphael Malbrue was growing up he had rabbits, fish, hermit crabs, hamsters, and dogs. He would have had more pets, but his parents decided five at one time was the limit. Even from a young age, he was never afraid of animals—not even snakes.

Today Raphael is a research veterinarian, which means he provides care for animals in research facilities, teaches courses to students, and does his own research.

Veterinarians must complete a four-year **post-baccalaureate degree**, but Raphel says hands-on experience in a vet clinic is also an asset. While cleaning kennels doesn't sound like fun, it's an important job. Kennel workers are often the first people to spot problems in an animal.

Whether a veterinarian works in a clinic or in a research facility, communication skills are essential. They have to talk to pet owners, support staff, and colleagues. Since the animals can't tell their doctor what is wrong, vets have to discuss symptoms and develop a course of action with the animal's owners. Seeing the bond between humans and

OTHER WORK

VETERINARIANS
can also be employed by:

★ Zoos

★ Aquariums

★ Aqua-culture farms

★ NASA (for animals used in space research)

★ Police forces, for forensic work relating to animals

PRO TIP

Dog-walking and pet-sitting are great ways to learn about animals and to get comfortable around them. If you can't be around animals, read about them. Make a top-ten list of the animals you'd like to get to know.

animals is one of the many rewarding parts of being a vet.

Raphael was mentored by some great vets as a science student, and today he returns the favor by advising students all the way from elementary to grad school. He also does outreach work in schools on behalf of the National Association for Black Veterinarians. And if you're not a fan of snakes, don't worry. He leaves them at home.

★ WHY NOT TRY ★

fostering at a local animal rescue agency. Taruna Daya was sixteen when she and her mom reached out to Manitoba Underdogs Rescue and offered to foster dogs who were waiting to be adopted. Since then, Taruna has had many dogs stay with her family, including a litter of puppies. Her work means the rescue dogs get experience in a home and are socialized, trained to walk on a leash, and taught some basic commands.

INSPIRING INDIVIDUALS

SAVANNAH HOWSE-SMITH and DR. DAYLE POITRAS-OSTER work at Rocky Rapids Veterinary Service, a mixed animal clinic in rural Alberta, Canada. They work with everything from tiny dogs to horses to injured owls. Along with a desire to help all animals, these two women bring something else to their practice: their Métis heritage. Understanding traditional Indigenous medicine and ways of doing things plays an important role in their work and is showcased in *Dr. Savannah: Wild Rose Vet*, the TV series about their clinic.

SPIN-OFF JOBS

★ Wildlife biologists studies animals and their behavior in natural habitats.

★ Epidemiologists are scientists who study diseases, many of which are zoonotic, which means they came from animals.

★ Large-animal veterinarians work with farms to care for livestock and are often based in rural settings.

JENNA HUTCHINSON & ASHLEY KOSOWAN

— Cake Designer / Entrepreneur • Graphic Artist / Entrepreneur —

" We get to be creative every day. "

When Jenna was a kid, she used to say that if she won the lottery, she'd open a bakery. Years later she and her twin sister Ashley have built a sweet empire in their hometown of Winnipeg.

Jenna's route to becoming a sought-after cake designer began with the TV show *Cake Boss*. Inspired by the creations she saw on the show, Jenna started baking and decorating cakes for family and friends. She loved the artistry of the process and didn't worry too much about the taste of the cakes—until she began getting orders from strangers. As her self-taught hobby became a business, Jenna learned to make her cakes taste as good as they looked.

While working on cakes might sound fun, it's also hard work. Because the cakes have to be fresh, Jenna often pulls

Other career options for **GRAPHIC DESIGNERS**:

OTHER WORK

★ **In-house graphic designers** develop and update the logo, website, brochures, and signage for one company.

★ **Freelance designers** work for themselves and are hired for specific projects.

★ **Salaried graphic designers** work with a team at marketing or advertising companies.

all-nighters, especially when she's working on a large cake for a wedding or event. Each cake is an advertisement for her business, so Jenna has to balance what the customer wants with her design **aesthetic**.

Just like Jenna, Ashley loves being creative. She discovered graphic design in a high-school course on advertising art, then went on to complete a three-year intensive graphic design course in college, followed by a hands-on internship. Her first job working for a wedding magazine gave her a strong skill set in typography, photo styling, art design, and layout.

Graphic designers need a keen eye for detail and an instinct for what looks good. Once Ashley and Jenna opened Jenna Rae Cakes, Ashley got to have a hand in everything to do with the look of the store, from the décor to the logo to the packaging.

A lot of Ashley's time is spent in front of a computer ensuring the visuals create a seamless, recognizable look that customers will associate with Jenna Rae Cakes. This all-inclusive approach to graphic design is called **branding**. The brand extends to social media, an important part of growing a business like theirs. In fact, Ashley says that posting on Instagram was great training. Paying attention to what customers reacted well to—whether it was color, font, or layout—helped the brand evolve.

Jenna and Ashley are not just talented in their creative professions; they're entrepreneurs too. With three bakeries, best-selling cookbooks, and more projects on the horizon, these two women have managed to blend their passion for design into sweet success.

SPIN-OFF JOBS

★ **Art directors** put magazines together and make sure text and images are appealing for the readers.

★ **Food stylists** make food look good on photo shoots for magazines, cookbooks, and advertisements.

RYAN WILSON

INSPIRING INDIVIDUALS

RYAN WILSON began baking when he received an Easy-Bake Oven for his eighth birthday. Three years later he was a contestant on the Food Network's *Kids Baking Championship* and then won the Cooking Channel's *Sugar Showdown*. Ryan is self taught and shares his expertise on his YouTube channel, *Baking with Ryan*, and on his Instagram account. Ryan's creations—from imposter cakes to rainbow frosting—rival those of much older bakers. Find him on Instagram at @ryanwilsonbakes

OMAR SACHEDINA

— Journalist —

> 66 I want to keep doing what I'm doing now. Traveling, telling stories, and learning. 99

Omar Sachedina's career in journalism started in sixth grade when a letter he wrote to the editor of his local newspaper was published. The discussion that followed showed him the value of being informed and engaged about the issues that mattered to him.

Omar grew up watching the news. He remembers going to the mosque on Friday nights and then coming home to watch a newsmagazine show. Omar liked learning about other places and asked a lot of questions. The news helped him make links between stories and understand the world better.

Throughout high school, Omar did a lot of writing. He also volunteered at radio stations to gain experience in the field. After getting a degree in political science, he moved to New York and received a master's in journalism. His first job as a TV reporter was in Timmins, Ontario.

★ WHY NOT TRY ★

Finding an issue that matters to you and writing a letter to the editor of a newspaper.

Journalism courses are available at both universities and community colleges. Media arts or communications programs focus on many areas of broadcasting so graduates can apply for entry-level jobs in journalism.

Journalists are trained to work in both print and broadcast media. Both involve tight deadlines and a responsibility to tell a story with honesty and compassion. Reporters have to deliver a fair, accurate, and unbiased account of events. They must tackle issues that matter to their community, even when the story is hard to tell.

A reporter's day is unpredictable. Omar starts by checking in with the assignment desk and discussing story ideas with other reporters. Then the chase starts. To get to the heart of a story, journalists must talk to the people who are involved. Omar will make calls and reach out to people he thinks will humanize the story for viewers. If he hits a dead end, he has to regroup and figure out a different approach.

Once the information is gathered, Omar will write up his report, listen to the interviews again, write a script for his on-air segment, and create an additional version of the story for online, all the while paying attention to unfolding events in case the information needs to be updated. After the story has been fact-checked, Omar can record what will be said over the video footage and film the on-camera segments. The timeline can be tight and the days are long, but you'd never know it by the polished presentation that appears on the evening news.

Being an effective communicator is an important part of being a journalist. So is versatility, because a journalist never knows where the story will take them. Journalists have to ask tough questions and be persistent. As Omar says, "It's okay to be the kid who asks 'why,' especially if it's an issue that matters to you."

SPIN-OFF JOBS

★ **Producers** work behind the scenes to find interviewees and video footage to help viewers understand the story.

★ **Camera operators** are needed both in the studio and on location. They help the journalist tell the story through visuals and need a good understanding of the equipment.

★ **Editors** put the story together. They revise and guide the journalists to ensure the story that needs to get told does.

LIVING the DREAM

CLARA LOPES SALIM is a kid reporter for Scholastic Kids Press. She lives in Brazil and says she loves "researching, interviewing, writing, and encouraging others to make change." One of her recent articles about the impact of an oil spill on baby sea turtles focused on community action and how people pitched in to relocate the turtle nests to areas not affected by the oil spill.

TIGER LILLI RUDGE

— Stuntperson / Stunt Coordinator —

> **❝** Being a stuntperson isn't about being a daredevil. It's about being smart. **❞**

Tiger Lilli never set out to be a stuntperson. She'd been working as a horse trainer and importer when a client connected her with her first stunt gig. Naturally athletic, and a bit of an adrenaline junkie, Tiger Lilli enjoyed using her knowledge of horses and trick riding skills in a different way. Her niche skill set got her a contract with a stunt agency and soon more stunting jobs were coming her way. Each new opportunity gave her the chance to learn from more experienced stuntpeople and gain new skills, like how to drive at high speeds or stage a fight scene.

Stuntpeople need to be good at lots of different things, like gymnastics, dance, martial arts, and using weapons. Additional skills like knowing how to rock climb or scuba dive will make you **marketable**. Stunt coordinators look for people who can follow choreography and move fluidly, so a dance or gymnastic background can help. Working well with a team is also essential.

A stuntperson's typical day on set begins with a detailed plan for what the director wants the stunt to look like. If the

FUN FACT

The highest-paid stunt was $100,000 for jumping off the CN Tower in Toronto in 1988. Dar Robinson fell nearly 1150 feet with no parachute—only a cable system he invented himself.

director doesn't have a specific vision, the stunt coordinator will make the decisions.

After working as a stuntperson for many years, Tiger Lilli became a stunt coordinator. In this role, she organizes action scenes that might have a cast of one or a hundred, and might be filmed on location or in a studio with a green screen. On very large projects, there might be a few stunt coordinators, each one responsible for certain scenes.

Stunt coordinators are responsible for everyone's safety and must enforce special precautions. If fire is involved, the fire department has to be on stand-by. Tiger Lilli has had some scary moments as a stuntperson. They've taught her to trust her gut and that she can never be too prepared.

As with any job in the film industry, there is the risk of having long breaks between jobs. Tiger Lilli kept her horse importation business for that reason, but stunt work is her passion. As someone who gets bored easily, she loves that every day is different. She loves pushing herself to do something that's never been done before and to do stunts in a new way. It's this flexible mindset that helps her pursue her ultimate goal: to be the first female to win an Oscar for Stunt Coordination.

INSPIRING INDIVIDUALS

Eager to get more Indigenous stunt performers involved in the entertainment industry, **MARTY WILDMAN CHIEFCALF** and **NATHANIEL ARCAND** started Canada's first Indigenous stunt school. At Stunt Nations, the veteran actors and stunt performers teach students how to do stunts like falling off horses and ladders, and how to choreograph their own fight scenes. Students get the chance to talk with Indigenous actors, and Elders share blessings with the students, empowering them to tackle an industry that often doesn't fairly represent Indigenous people.

BLAKE BOLDEN

— NHL Scout —

❝ Be bold. ❞

When hockey legend Luc Robitaille told Blake Bolden she had the right skill set to be a professional scout, she listened.

She was well equipped for the job. Blake has been involved in hockey since she was six years old. Before she became a scout, she played professional hockey for the Canadian Women's Hockey League, the National Women's Hockey League (today called the Premier Hockey Federation), and in Switzerland with HC Lugano. Blake's background as a player, mentor, and coach has helped her, but what matters most for scouts is a strong work ethic and a love of the game. Some scouts work their way up by connecting with coaches and team managers to alert them to new talent. If these tips prove to be reliable, a scout's reputation grows and a team might consider hiring them. In Blake's case, Luc Robitaille could tell she'd be a great fit for the Los Angeles Kings.

Scouting also means a lot of travel and, of course, a lot of hockey. Blake tries to watch as many games as possible. She's always got a list of players and prospects she's keeping tabs on. During a game, she takes careful notes that she later inputs into a spreadsheet. It's not just about finding the fastest skater, or the player with the best shot. A lot of **metrics** go into making a team. She has to consider salary caps, trades, player contracts, and the team as a whole.

Blake works closely with her team's general manager, who makes the ultimate decision on who will be asked to join the team. Considerations include which dominant hand a player uses, what position he plays, if he's a defensive or

★ WHY NOT TRY ★

Joining a fantasy league for your favorite sport.

PRO TIP

Check out some junior-level hockey in your area. You never know, you might be watching the next top draft pick!

a power forward, as well as other "intangible metrics" like competitiveness and attitude. Basically, she has to predict what a 20-year-old player will be like in five or six years, and whether his skills and attitude make him a good fit for her team.

Knowledge of the game is essential, but there are other skills that make Blake a good scout. She's organized and, thanks to years of playing hockey, is used to being prepared. Communicating well is also important as Blake represents her team during negotiations and contract talks.

Scouting for a professional sports team is definitely a non-traditional job, especially for a woman. Ultimately, she sees her diversity as a positive because it speaks to the inclusivity of her team—something that's helpful when she's recruiting new players. Blake would like to continue the work she's started with the LA Kings, watching them grow and finding ways to make room for herself within the organization. Along the way, there is no doubt she'll be holding the door open to others as well.

LIVING the DREAM

At 14, JONATHAN KYRIACOU decided he had a brighter future as a hockey scout than as a AAA player. He applied to intern with a hockey sports agency and was lucky enough to land it. Hard work and dedication led him to other opportunities: he worked as a scout for the OHL's Ottawa 67's and then as a hockey operations intern for the Toronto Maple Leafs.

SPIN-OFF JOBS

★ **Analysts** track and record players' statistics. They help scouts, coaches, and general managers create the best team possible.

★ **Detectives** pay attention to clues and follow leads, just like a hockey scout. They also have to keep organized notes and carefully log information.

★ **General managers** handle a team's contracts for players and coaches. They often do media briefings and may be the spokesperson for the team.

FUN FACT

Some areas are considered "hockey hot spots", such as Minnesota, Michigan, and Massachusetts in the US, and all of Canada. Scouts spend more time looking at players in these geographic areas.

WEDAD AMIRI
— Clothing Designer —

> 66 Believe in your product and go for it! 99

When Wedad Amiri couldn't find a dress to wear to a family event, she jokingly told her mom that she should make her own. Wedad hadn't studied fashion design and had only basic sewing skills, but she didn't let that stop her. She drew a design of what she wanted, contacted a seamstress, and hired her to make two skirts. When people started asking where she'd bought her clothes, Wedad realized she was onto something.

As a Muslim woman, Wedad wanted modest outfits that were stylish and showed her personality. Based on the feedback she got, other people did too. Wedad began to think about making her hobby into a business. She got samples made of her designs, found models, and sold tickets to a fashion show. In one evening she sold all the clothes and had orders for more!

Wedad wants to change the narrative for Muslim people and put a fashion-forward face to what it means to be Muslim. Having worked with mental-health initiatives in her previous job, Wedad decided that her business, Afflatus Hijab, would be about more than just designing and selling clothes.

While Wedad is self-taught, many programs offer diplomas and degrees in fashion design. Courses like fashion sketching, pattern making, construction, and draping teach students how to make their designs come to life. Internships let aspiring designers study under seasoned professionals, and to gain experience in different workplaces—from mainstream, mass-produced clothing to high-end **haute couture**.

SHARING CULTURE

Rankin Inlet, Nunavut is a long way from New York City, but Nunavummiut **VICTORIA KAKUKTINNIQ** didn't let a few thousand miles stop her. She started her fashion line at twenty-one years old after learning traditional sewing from elders in her community and completing a fashion design program in Winnipeg, Manitoba. Victoria moved to Iqaluit where she started her company, Victoria's Arctic Fashion. Victoria's designs are inspired by traditional amautik worn by Inuit women, nature, and the colors of the Arctic. In 2020, she traveled to New York City for her first New York Fashion Week.

She focuses on destigmatizing mental health and empowers women by highlighting the strength of Indigenous women, single mothers, and refugees through her designs. She even names pieces in each collection after inspiring women.

Wedad initially struggled with the lack of structure and routine that come with **self-employment**, but now she loves that she can plan her own days. She is in charge of the website, marketing, social media, order fulfillment, inventory management, and events, including fashion shows and pop-up stores. She also designs new lines for each season to keep her customers interested. All Wedad's hard work paid off when she was invited to New York Fashion Week. What started as a joke with her mom has grown into a successful and respected business with a bright future.

SPIN-OFF JOBS

★ **Visual merchandisers** design the layout of a store, including window and mannequin displays.

★ **Personal stylists** help people put together outfits, organize wardrobes, and plan future fashion purchases.

★ **Retail buyers** are responsible for the products you see in stores. They attend fashion shows, meet with suppliers, and decide which items fit their store brand.

LIVING the DREAM

EGYPT 'IFY' UFELE started a fashion business at age eleven. Frustrated because the clothes sold for curvy kids just weren't flattering or fashionable, she used the skills she'd learned to sew for her Barbie dolls to make her own clothing. Word spread quickly about her fashion line, which she named ChubiiLine, and about the special kid behind the designs. Ify became the youngest person to show at New York Fashion Week. She has gone on to win multiple awards for her work as a role model and a leader.

KRISTINE BYERS

— Carpenter —

> " Innovate. There's not any one way to build. "

Even though Kristine loved to putter in the garage with her dad and asked for a scroll saw, a type of power tool, for her twelfth birthday, she never thought of a **trade**, like carpentry, as a career until later. After high school, she went to the Royal Military College of Canada and studied engineering for a year before deciding the hands-on work of carpentry was more rewarding.

Kristine took a six-month course at a technical college to learn the foundations like joinery (furniture building) and carpentry (making or building with wood). She fell in love with the creative work of joinery, but there were more opportunities in carpentry, so that was the direction she followed.

Trade or technical colleges like Kristine's alternate class work with **apprenticeships**. For the next four years, she rotated between in-class training from an instructor and on-the-job training as an apprentice. After she completed her technical

FUN FACT

The term *journeyperson* originated in the Middle Ages. People who worked in trades were paid daily. The word *journey* is derived from the French word *journée*, which means day.

OTHER WORK

CARPENTERS can work in a few fields:

★ Industrial carpentry involves big infrastructure jobs like bridges, mines, and grain silos.

★ Commercial carpenters build the foundation for roofs and staircases, as well as the interior framing and flooring for houses and buildings.

★ Set carpenters work in film and TV.

training and her required hours, she got her **journey ticket** and became a **journeyperson**.

As a journeyperson, Kristine was part of a site crew. Their leader would set out their goals and assign tasks to each member of the crew. If a problem arose, the team would talk it over to reach a solution.

After working as a journeyperson, Krisine passed her **Red Seal** exam. A Red Seal is an inter-provincial qualification that allows a carpenter to practice their trade throughout Canada. In the United States, each state has its own **certification** program. With her Red Seal, Kristine could now run crews and teach.

Currently an instructor, Kristine is eager to share her skills. She's been involved with specialized programs, like one that trained ten Gitxaala Nation members, four of whom were women, to become carpenter apprentices. Kristine gives back in other ways too. She worked with other trades to repair a women's shelter in Vancouver and supports programs that promote women in trades. She says that eighty percent of the skills a carpenter needs are learned on site, through trial and error. She tells her students that they can't really fail because they're always going to learn something, even if it's the wrong way to do something.

SHARING KNOWLEDGE

Growing up, **CHUCK COMMANDA** often helped his grandparents build traditional Algonquin canoes at their home in Kitigan Zibi, an Anishinabeg First Nation community in Quebec. Today he shares that knowledge as a master canoe builder. Chuck harvests the cedar wood, spruce needles, and birch bark himself, taking only what is needed. Whether Chuck is working in a school, a museum, or a community, the lessons he shares go beyond just woodworking. Building a canoe is about sharing the Sacred Grandfather Teachings of love, wisdom, bravery, courage, humility, honesty, and truth.

SPIN-OFF JOBS

★ **Civil engineers** often work with architects and carpenters on large construction projects like roads, buildings, airports, and bridges.

★ **Millwrights** install and repair machinery in powerplants and factories. They are also called industrial mechanics.

★ **Furniture designers** combine function and fashion as they design pieces for peoples' homes. Many designers use carpentry skills to build prototypes of their creations.

CHUCK COMMANDA

STEPHANIE HARVEY

— Professional Video Game Player / Gaming Expert —

> 66 I train like any
> other professional competitor. 99

Stephanie, or missharvey as she's known in the gaming world, has been at the forefront of the industry since it began. Twenty years ago, when Stephanie started playing video games for fun, she didn't know it would lead her to being a *Counter-Strike* world champion. Or that she would transfer her success playing the game to working behind the scenes as a game developer.

Becoming a world champion didn't happen by accident. Stephanie worked hard to develop her skill set. There were some days when she didn't feel like playing, but she knew she had to log the hours in order to get better and keep her skills sharp.

Stephanie practiced for four to five hours a day in a scrimmage with players from other gaming teams. With her own squad, she analyzed strategies and ran through potential scenarios to get better. Her coach watched her play and found areas where she could improve. Coaches are a new role in gaming, but they are essential to ensure healthy team dynamics and collaboration in the competitive gaming world.

When Stephanie was an **amateur**, she received no financial support. She had to pay her own way to travel and enter tournaments. As she won, she gained a following. This led to bigger tournaments and more prize money. It took fifteen years, but eventually Stephanie realized that she could turn her passion into a real job.

With all Stephanie's experience in the gaming world, it made sense for her to transition into game development.

SPIN-OFF JOBS

★ **Architects** design buildings in the real world.

★ **3-D animators** create the visual images in a game.

★ **Video game testers** play the games to catch glitches before the game is released to the public.

Her career as a world champion helps her see the game from the player's perspective. She's always looking at how to achieve the optimal player experience.

As a game developer, Stephanie worked with her team, which included programmers, animators, and concept artists, to bring the game to life. Once a prototype was ready, Stephanie would try it out. If she and her team liked it, they kept working to refine it and add details.

Stephanie is currently the director of business development at Counter Logic Gaming (CLG), an esports organization where she used to play professionally. Stephanie uses her experience in professional esports and game development to advocate for healthy gaming and diversity in esports.

Game development is a growing field. Some middle and high schools use video games in class and teach coding. Stephanie says that in her industry, people who know how to code are always a step ahead.

Stephanie calls the video gaming world an "ecosystem," and it's a good term to use. It's an industry that is constantly growing and changing. She wants to promote more diversity in gaming and encourage more girls to start competing—the earlier the better.

MAKING a DIFFERENCE

With the belief that video games can drive social justice, Games for Change (G4C) challenges students to create games that promote real-world change based on themes ranging from resilience to sustainability to advocating for animals or making cities accessible for all people. The winning games are available for play on their website, **gamesforchange.org**.

FUTURE DREAM JOBS

Have you ever dreamed of flying a spaceship?
How about bringing back an extinct species?
While these jobs sound unusual in the present,
they might not be in the future.

★ Space Pilot ★

As we move from commercial airplanes to commercial spacecraft, we'll need trained pilots to fly them. With knowledge of astrophysics, astronomy, and engineering, this will be an out-of-this-world job for some people.

★ Extinct Species Revivalist ★

It is estimated that 200–2000 species die off each year. Imagine if we could use technology to reverse these losses. Harvesting DNA of endangered species could prevent extinctions and reintroduce species to their natural habitats. An understanding of biology, chemistry, and medicine will be important.

★ Companion for the Aged ★

As people live longer, the need for assistance will be greater. Companions who can run errands with the elderly, provide company and care, and help to keep them in their homes will be important. If you are a good communicator and have patience and empathy, this could be the job for you.

★ AI Specialist ★

Many people believe that artificial intelligence, or AI, will be commonplace in the future. An AI specialist is someone who uses their knowledge of engineering, programming, and computer science to guide the technology.

★ Sustainable Energy Technician ★

As people change their habits and turn to renewable energy, the demand for expertise in how to collect and distribute wind, solar, and geothermal energy will be important. Engineering skills and environmental and meteorological training will be needed.

★ Commercial Drone Pilots ★

They might seem like fun toys, but drones have a lot of potential. Knowing how to fly them is a useful skill. Whether drones are used for deliveries, to shoot aerial photography, or to conduct geographic research, drone pilots will be sought after. An understanding of technology and aeronautics will be essential.

★ Urban Agricultural Specialists ★

It is predicted that by 2050, 5.2 billion people will be city dwellers. In order for cities to be sustainable, systems will need to be put in place for food to be grown inside their borders. Urban agricultural specialists who can use hydroponics and vertical farming methods will be in high demand.

DEVELOP THE SKILL SET

Every job requires certain skills to do it well. **Technical skills** are the ones you gain through training. They can be learned on the job, through a mentor, or at a secondary institution like a trade school or university. Examples of technical skills are: using programming languages, mastering particular software, or operating power tools.

Technical skills are usually specific to a career or industry.

Soft skills relate to the way you behave with other people. They include communication, teamwork, dependability, organization, growth mindset, and flexibility.

Soft skills are transferable across careers and industries.

Here are some ways to train your soft skills:

★ Communication ★
Speak up in class, join clubs, or volunteer at jobs where you interact with the public.

★ Problem solving ★
Build things, fix things, or try puzzles that encourage teamwork, like escape rooms. These activities build confidence and give you experience thinking outside the box.

★ Creativity ★
Find a new way to solve a common problem, devise an original plan to raise funds for a charity, or suggest ways to improve your school.

★ Adaptability ★
When things don't go your way, consider what might be a positive outcome. Hockey game got canceled? If the ice is free, suggest an extra practice or a game of road hockey with your team.

ACKNOWLEDGMENTS / PHOTO CREDITS

This book was made possible thanks to all the inspiring people who agreed to share their stories with us. **Thank you!**

Along the way, we reached out to others for more information. Thank you to the following experts: Tasha Bergen, Angie Kennedy, and Niles Johnson.

As always, a special thank-you to the team who work behind the scenes. Much gratitude to Erin Alladin for being a dream editor and also for her patience with our never-ending questions; Gail Winskill for loving the idea of this book as much as we did; Lorena González Guillén for designing it and bringing the pages to life with her masterful layouts; Angelo Cruz for his work in production; and the whole Pajama Press team for marketing and promoting it. A special thank-you to Scot Ritchie for the illustrations that brought that extra bit of sparkle to the pages.

Photo Credits

Page 8: Melissa Márquez © Freddie Claire | Page 9: Riley Hathaway © Richard Robinson | Page 10: Sunil Gurmukh © Monica Gurmukh | Page 17: Neijae Graham-Henries © Katerina Christina | Page 18: Brenda Hsueh © Skyler Radojkovic | Page 20: Mark Robinson © Daniel Shaw | Page 22: Scott Edwards © Beth Adams | Page 23: Mya-Rose Craig © Oliver Edwards | Page 27: Amoy Antunet © Creative Soul | Page 38: Joshua Jones © Jenny Jimenez | Page 40: Christa Bruneau-Guenther © Gabrielle Touchette Photography | Page 44: Jenna Hutchinson & Ashley Kosowan © Brittany Mahood

GLOSSARY

A

academics: educational courses, especially of higher learning

accolades: an award or expression of admiration

accredited: to be officially recognized

aesthetic: a design's pleasing quality

amateur: a person does work but is unpaid

apprentice: a person who is learning a trade from a skilled individual

apprenticeship: a period of training in which an apprentice learns a trade

B

baccalaureate degree: a degree given to a student who has completed (usually) four years of study at a college or university. Also known as a bachelor's degree

biodiversity: the wide variety of life on earth

branding: distinctive wording or design used to identify a particular brand

C

contract: an agreement that states the terms of employment

certification: an official document proving a level of achievement

D

data: a collection of facts

degenerative: describing something that declines or deteriorates

degree: a title given to a student upon completion of an academic program

E

entrepreneur: a person who operates their own business

F

faculty: a group of university departments focused on one area of knowledge

food insecurity: the lack of stable access to enough food

G

graduate: a person who has successfully completed a course

H

haute couture: expensive, hand-made clothes produced by leading fashion houses

I

internship: a period in which a student or trainee works, sometimes without pay, to gain experience

J

journeyperson: a person who has learned a trade

journey ticket: a certificate of qualification to become a journeyperson

M

marketable: in demand

master's degree: an academic degree given to a person who has demonstrated a mastery of a specific field of study

mentor: an experienced and trusted advisor

metrics: assessments used to compare and track performance

N

neurodegenerative: related to the breakdown of nervous tissue

neurotransmitters: a substance that transmits nerve impulses

P

pH level: the amount of an acid or base in a liquid

PhD: abbreviation for Doctor of Philosophy, the highest academic degree a person can get in a field of study

post-baccalaureate degree: a program that is not a graduate degree but requires a baccalaureate, or bachelor's, degree for entry

post-doctorate fellow: someone who is continuing their research or training after completing a PhD

practicum: the hands-on part of a course of study

prodigy: a young person with exceptional abilities

professor: a teacher at a university or college

R

Red Seal: the highest level of certification a tradesperson in Canada can possess

retinal: relating to the retina, which is the sensory membrane of the eye

rookie: a new recruit in their first year

S

scholarship: a grant given to support a student's education, usually awarded because of academic or other achievement

scientific method: an organized way to think about and solve problems based on data

self-employment: working for yourself, instead of an employer

T

technical (or trade) school: a facility that teaches the technical knowledge and practical skills needed for a particular job

topography: the natural or man-made features of a place or region

trade: a skilled job requiring special training

U

undergraduate degree: see baccalaureate

university: an academic institution with many branches of learning

INDEX